From the Projects to a Ph.D.

A View from the Other Side of America

Dr. Vanessa Howard

Howard Univer-City, LLC
Maryland Heights, Missouri

This book is a work of nonfiction. These accounts are from the author's perspective and memories, and as such, are represented as accurately and faithfully as possible. To maintain the anonymity of the individuals involved, some of the names and details have been changed.

Howard Univer-City, LLC
12685 Dorsett Road PMB 225
Maryland Heights, MO 63043-2380

Cover Designed by: J.L Woodson: www.woodsoncreativestudio.com
Interior Designed by: Lissa Woodson: www.naleighnakai.com
Editors: J. L. Campbell www.joylcampbell.com
Lissa Woodson: www.naleighnakai.com

PRINTED IN THE UNITED STATES OF AMERICA
ISBN 978-1-7366987-0-9

From the Projects to a Ph.D.

A View from the Other Side of America

Dr. Vanessa Howard

To my daughters, Laura Howard and Faye Collins, and my
granddaughter, Nala.
I wrote this story for you because you were my inspiration
to change, learn, and grow. Your love encouraged me to push
past my fears and taught me that the only limitations I have
in my life are the ones I create for myself. You guys have
taught me to take the restrictions off my life, and you opened
my heart to believe in myself again.

◆ ACKNOWLEDGEMENTS ◆

Writing this book was harder than I could have imagined, and yet therapeutic enough to bring clarity to my life. It was written to inspire and uplift the human spirit. Many times, I am asked by my non-African American friends or colleagues to speak for the African American community or to share the African American's viewpoint on an issue. I always feel inadequate when called to speak for all African Americans because one person cannot generalize the African American experience. Each person's understanding is unique to the blueprint of their life. My goal in writing this book was to share personal insights and happenings that shaped me as an individual. Although the scenarios shared in this book are not unique to one person, the examples that are revealed provide a glimpse into the other side of America which is rarely shared with other cultures. My prayer is that my story can be a catalyst for change and hope.

I want to thank God, my Creator, for providing me with life issues that shaped and molded me into the person I have become. At my lowest points when I became overwhelmed with the issues of life, You gave me the strength to persevere. When I had a stroke in 2013, my language became delayed and my thinking was jumbled, You said, "I'm not done with you yet."

After my stroke, You blessed me to be promoted to Teacher of the Year for one of the largest school districts in the state of Missouri, elevated me to become an Elementary School Principal of over 600 students, and ultimately helped me earn my doctorate degree. Thank you for keeping me from becoming a statistic because of my humble beginnings.

Thank you to my church family, Lively Stone Church of God, for your prayers and support. To my pastors, the late Bishop Alphonso Scott, and Bishop Lee Scott, for encouraging me to write a book.

Many thanks to the late Bishop Alphonso Scott for giving me a pen to sign checks that I would earn from my literary experiences.

I could not have completed From Projects to a Ph.D. without mentors who shared their expertise with me. Ms. Lola Thomas, Mrs. Robin Witherspoon, Ms. Suzette Simms, Mr. Ralph Moore, Dr. JoAnn Clay, Mrs. Mona Dougherty, Mrs. Kimberly Gillingham, and Dr. Shelia Ward, I appreciate your mentorship that shaped my professional journey.

A special thanks to Lissa Woodson (Naleighna Kai) the Book Whisperer, who inspired me to join the 30-Day Writing Challenge. Thank you for providing guidance through the book writing process. Thanks also for selecting Shakir Rashaan as my writing coach. Shakir helped me persevere when I wanted to quit.

To J. L. Woodson, thank you for your creative insights in developing my cover. I am also grateful to my editors, J. L. Campbell and Janice Allen, for helping me to keep my author's voice through the editing process. Thank you to the Tribe of writers for becoming my support system and my second family. Thank you, guys, for your editorial help, keen insight, and ongoing support in bringing my story to life. It is because of the Tribe's combined efforts and encouragement that I have a living and breathing legacy that is now shared with the world.

To my family, in particular: my brother, Donald Wesley, for always being the person that I could turn to during my darkest times and years of despair. Your words of wisdom gave me the strength to pick myself up every time I fell. To my mother, the late Lillie Johnson, for giving birth to me and instilling the importance of education. I love you, and we did this book together. To my daughters, Laura, and Faye, for being understanding and supportive as I pursued my dreams. Thank you for loving me even when my work and ambitions took me away from spending quality time with you. To my granddaughter, Nala, for being my inspiration to leave you a legacy. I can't wait to see what God has planned for you.

Finally, to all those who have been a part of my getting to this point: Pastor Jerome & Granotta Farquharson, Pastor Vera Tyus, Elder Donna Mosley, Evangelist Tammy Dees, Mother Maxine Moore, Uncle Frank & Aunt Odessa Lester. I love you more than words can express. I appreciate all my family and friends who have spoken words of blessings over my life.

I am mature and menopausal, so charge any name omissions to my mind and not to my heart.

Dr. Vanessa Howard

Our sin was locked in our skin. Cruelty stained the very air we breathed. The odds were stacked against us in towers of glass and stone. We weren't meant to survive. We were built to last. The brilliance beneath our skin is the jewel in our crown and the cornerstone of our empire. For every brick thrown, perseverance is the mortar. Disadvantages are the cobblestones we walk on. We were meant for greater things, more than even we could possibly imagine.

Stephanie M. Freeman, Author of Necessary Evil and Nature of the Beast

Chapter 1:

CHASING THE WHITE CLOUD

After earning my doctorate degree, my daughter, Alice, made the comment, "From the Projects to a Ph.D."

These simple words transformed this fifty-plus-year-old lady into a two-year-old. In an instant, a flashback emerged of my younger self walking amongst the concrete palaces that St. Louis called the Projects. Sweltering heat radiating from the gray concrete pierced the soles of my feet. Wow, I almost forgot about life in the projects in the 1960s.

That memory shifted into a mental picture of a group of children chasing a white cloud. A truck drove through the projects, spraying as it went along. Sometimes workers wearing silver suits would spray white clouds from the rooftops. I imagined that they were astronauts spraying moon dust to cool us off. The sheer semi-liquid haze provided temporary relief to our hot bodies.

I would run as fast as my little legs would let me; however, I could never catch that white cloud. Its mists left white fairy dust on our clothing. We didn't mind having to shake off the tiny particles as we enjoyed the cool dew. We would simply brush the fine particles off our clothing and return to our games. The whirling sound of the double Dutch rope clapping on the concrete would resume when those clouds dissipated.

My memories of living in the projects are in black and white, like old photographs and sometimes video clips. The recollections had neither sequence nor order. Nine people were in my family. I was an only daughter, with six older brothers. My dad refused to get food stamps or any other type of governmental assistance. He wanted to support the family with the resources that he earned because, *"That's what men do."*

My parents made the difficult decision to move us to the projects. Our new location would ensure that our basic needs would be met. The projects were government-subsidized housing for impoverished people. Strategically placed in an area of St. Louis, they isolated low-income families. In the 1960s, two types of housing existed: high rise or single level. My family chose the single level housing.

Essential needs of clothing, food, and shelter were met, so it didn't appear that my family was in a low-income bracket. Entertainment came from the simple things in life: marbles, army men, dolls, and Legos.

Ms. America had nothing on this girl. Everyone was my friend. I wandered through the projects with the naivety of a toddler. Asking a lot of questions and waving to people around me was my norm. The innocent mistake of a child's friendliness caused me to receive many slaps on my hand from my parents. No one explained the rationale for not talking to strangers, so my natural behavior was transformed into silent waves. This was the start of my people-watching skills. Asking questions for clarity is still my method of operation. It's truly ironic that my professional career would consist of asking and answering questions.

My family walked to Soulard Farmer's Market, a public facility in St. Louis, and the only one operated by the city government. It might be one of the oldest public markets in the United States, west of the Mississippi River. Farmers had booths where they sold produce, meat, and other items at very affordable prices. My mom made weekly trips to this market. A master at bargaining, she purchased the most amount of food she could, while spending the least amount of money. I enjoyed watching her tell vendors, "That price is too high. I can find that item cheaper if I keep walking."

Sometimes the vendors would call her back and give her the price she wanted. If they didn't give her the best deal, she made good on her threat and kept walking until she could purchase something within her budget.

The smell of fresh produce, especially the citrusy aroma of oranges and lemons, was intoxicating. The vibrant colors of the fruit and vegetable displays kept me mesmerized, trying to figure out each farmers' patterns. The simple things in life teach the greatest lessons. Understanding patterns would prepare me for learning complex number concepts and mathematical operations.

The highlight of our visit to Soulard Market was the playground area, and mom would let us eat a piece of fruit as we played on the swings. I loved the sound of the wind whizzing by my ears while I swung high in the air. Once it was time to walk home, Mom made each child carry something. The heavy brown paper bags made the trip laborious.

In the summertime, the project's concrete buildings and sidewalks seemed to pull the sun's sweltering heat closer to the ground. We didn't have shade from the radiating heat. When we played outside, there was no protection from the sun's hot rays.

The projects didn't have any social outlets for children to channel their young energy. Fighting and playing together were the two ways that we interacted with each other until the white cloud came.

The white cloud was the one unifying factor in the projects. The cool, white mist brought much needed relief from the exhausting heat. As children, we didn't understand the purpose or plan behind this weekly drizzle. All we knew was that a team would periodically spray the projects with the cooling haze. Unlike the similar ritual that other children in affluent neighborhoods had, being lured by the music of the ice cream trucks, our white cloud graced us with its presence and brought a whimsical peace. We didn't fight each other; we had one unifying objective, and that was to find relief from the scorching, concrete. Years later, the true and deadly essence of the cloud was revealed.

The residents of St. Louis Projects were predominantly African American. The military sponsored chemical spraying in impoverished areas of St. Louis in the 1950s and 1960s. St. Louis was among several test cities chosen by government contractors for spraying zinc cadmium sulfide, a chemical powder mixed with fluorescent particles. St. Louis was chosen because it had a similar appearance to some of the Russian cities. The United States government thought these were possible attack sites. The spray was part of a biological weapons program. Local officials were told that the government was testing a smokescreen which could shield St. Louisans from an attack from Russia.

Can you believe St. Louis City officials agreed to this without *any type* of investigation? Why were the projects used for testing? Did the projects really look like a Russian city or was there a more sinister plot brewing? The secret testing used by the federal government was revealed to Congress in 1994. Missouri House Resolution No. 58 acknowledged the events that occurred.

The Missouri House Resolution acknowledged that the United States Army sprayed chemical agents over thousands of unsuspecting residents without their knowledge. Most of the residents were low-income African Americans, and 70% was comprised of children under the age of twenty-one. My siblings and I were exposed to this dangerous element for four years.

The House Resolution confirmed that the testing was conducted throughout the Pruit-Igoe Housing Projects. The United States Army spread zinc cadmium sulfide using blowers perched atop of the low-income housing buildings and schools. The United States Army didn't notify local politicians about the content of the testing. The true purpose wasn't revealed until Congress led the inquest in 1994.

My mother had the foresight to know that her family needed to leave the projects. She prayed and believed that God would direct her path. My dad had a sixth-grade education, and my mom didn't complete high school. Even with the educational deficits, Mom knew that education was the key to improving our living situation. She returned to school to train to become a nurse's assistant.

While raising seven young children, she worked full-time tirelessly as a domestic maid, using public transportation to get around. Although, Mom had limited reading abilities, she successfully completed her coursework to become a nurse's assistant. Then she saved a thousand dollars for the down payment to purchase a house.

Years later, when the public became aware of the true nature of the white cloud in the projects, I questioned my mother about it. The information that the families were given was that they were spraying the projects for mosquitoes. Why did my mom blindly trust the city's reason for spraying our neighborhood? Why did parents allow the children to run behind the trucks if they were spraying insecticide?

My Mom told me she wasn't aware that her daughter had been running behind the truck or playing in the insecticide spray. This was likely true because whenever the screen door was unlocked, I escaped and wandered around the community. Most of the time my getaways went unnoticed.

The more questions asked, the more irritated my mom became.

Why was she being so dismissive with me?

The conversation ended because she was so uncomfortable. In hindsight, her irritation was rooted in the thought of discovering that her family was in danger. She blindly trusted the government's sinister experiment on human test subjects that included her children. She didn't want to discuss the matter.

I began reading newspaper articles and court cases to get more information. It still astonishes me that experimental radioactive particles were freely disbursed in the projects. No thought was given about the repercussions to my community. Some of the residents developed lung issues or cancers because of what the government did. Thirty-plus years later, several residents unsuccessfully filed lawsuit. It would have been nice to have civil rights activist Erin Brockovich's support.

Black people mistrust the scientific world because of human rights betrayals like this and the Tuskegee Syphilis Experiment. In these two incidents, African Americans seemed to be America's Guinea pigs. I can relate to that inherent misgivings because it happened in my lifetime and was part of my experience. Our doubtfulness stems from historical events and has been reinforced by health system issues and discriminatory events that continue to this day. As our nation tries to eradicate and slow down Covid-19, I am cautious about accepting the vaccination because of my white cloud experience.

Mistrust of science and governmental authorities can seem foreign to anyone who has not received this type of immoral treatment. My family could have been a statistic from the aftermath of being exposed to radioactive materials. In fact, because of my mom, Dr. V *is* a statistic, but in a more positive way. Less than 2% of the world's population has a doctorate. According to the U.S. Census Bureau, only 1.2% of the US population has a PhD. This lady is blessed to be in the Ph.D. statistic and still alive. What would have happened if we stayed in the projects longer? The white cloud could have been my demise.

Chapter 2:

HOW DO YOU SPEND $20,000 IN A YEAR?

Busted, broke, and disgusted, my dream was flickering in the wind.
Spring 2016 was the start of my doctoral program. Weeks into the
semester, the financial aid department notified me the funds needed for
classes was denied. Determined not to abandon my dream, I started
corresponding with university departments to see if scholarships were
available, or even if they could refer me to a resource. My efforts were
futile, even with seeking outside resources and other scholarships. No
one could help me. They sympathized with my plight, however, couldn't
provide any financial assistance.

Sharing my aspirations with my friends seemed like the wrong thing
to do. What would be my next steps in this dilemma?

My last hope was to make a payment arrangement. Talking to
a representative only led to me being told it would be impossible to

make one that would be satisfactory for the university. Determined to finish my coursework, the only option was to continue making requests to whomever would listen. Ms. Jones, the financial aid director, was the person I relentlessly contacted by phone and email, until my correspondences became a gnat buzzing in her ear.

Finally, a payment plan was offered to me. According to the arrangement, $1700 was due no later than the fifth of each month for two years. This payment was in addition to my regular living expenses. These bills included rent, car note, utilities, car insurance, etc. And you know a girl must look good, so hair and nails had to be done bi-weekly. Dressing for success in heels was my method of operation. Walking into a room, individuals glanced at my outfits with approving looks. The intricate designs on my nails received frequent compliments. Dressing in this manner was a duty, as it gave students that looked like me a professional role model.

This dilemma took the wind from underneath my wings and landed me face down with mud on my face. As my former pastor put it, "Man's extremities are God's opportunities to show up and show out." Now it was time to put my faith into action and depend on God to make a way. Didn't He do it for Abraham? Well, my ram was somewhere, and with patience, God would reveal His plan to me and show me how to navigate these financial waters.

In the meantime, I had to activate my faith to do the doggone thing. This uphill battle was on and popping. Growing up, the preachers always said, '*Faith is the substance of things hoped for, and the evidence of things not seen.*' Well, Lord, help thou my unbelief and show me how to get this accomplished. *Amen.*

The reality of my situation was that I had limited money in my budget to fulfill a dream. Signing the payment arrangement was a great leap of faith. Personal financial adjustments had to be made to accomplish my goal. Ms. Jones reiterated that this agreement was against her better judgement. My payment plan had to be notarized so that the university could secure the debt. This was done for each semester of attendance.

Many personal sacrifices were made. Trips to the hairdresser were the first thing to be eliminated. My budget could no longer support two-hundred-dollar Malaysian hair weaves plus sew-in fees. A synthetic wig cost thirty-five dollars and it lasted two-to-three months before needing to be replaced.

There is a great difference between synthetic and human hair. Synthetic wigs can hold styles better after washing or even after a walk in the rain. Human-hair weave is made from real human hair, so they look and feel real. However, they must be re-styled after washing, like real hair. Synthetic hair is not heat friendly, which means that it can melt or get matted because of heat or high humidity. Can you imagine going on a candlelight romantic meal and realizing that the thing that is cooking is your hair?

Next, getting manicures and pedicures every two weeks was scratched off my schedule. Wearing overlays for years had caused my natural nails to weaken and become paper thin. They were cracked and brittle. Let's not talk about my feet. Desperate to wear sandals in the summer, DIY (do it yourself) pedicure became the only choice. My attempts were disastrous. Let's just say my feet looked a hot mess. Sandals were no longer an option because bear paws should never be visible in the daytime.

My eating habits also had to change. As a single lady with no children at home, I am the sole person on the financial agenda. Readjusting to a limited budget required me to purchase Ramen noodles, rice, bags of frozen vegetables, and a bag of chicken wings, to conserve funds.

At that time, my employment was at a central office in one of the largest school districts in Missouri. Eating out was a luxury and a pleasurable distraction for our highly stressful positions. One day, my friend, Sarah, saw my lunch and yelled, "Hey y'all. Vanessa's eating Ramen noodles."

I waved at her and said, "Girl, don't knock it. You know every now and then, you eat Ramen noodles, too. They taste good and remind me of my college days."

Eating in the lounge with the staff became uncomfortable because purchasing lunch daily was no longer in my budget. My car was now my place of refuge, where I could eat in peace and recharge myself. I listened to inspirational music, read textbooks, and completed research for my dissertation. This helped me become more productive with my limited time.

Tuition payment became an annoying companion that never left my side. I named it Jack. He was tall, dark, but not at all handsome. My actual installment due date was the first of every month. If payment wasn't received by the fifth, I would automatically be withdrawn from my classes. My new boarder got his nickname of *Jack* in honor of the Ray Charles's song "Hit the Road, Jack." Jack was going to get kicked out in two years.

The school district paid employees twice a month. My first check of the month was used to pay my living expenses, rent, plus late fees. The last check for the month was used for tuition. Using creative budgeting, utility bills were paid right before they were scheduled to be disconnected.

I stayed the course, and two years later made that final payment as planned. Amid celebrating my personal accomplishment, I never imagined receiving backhanded compliments. Some of my colleagues and friends would choke as if they had a hair ball stuck in their throat when referring to me as Dr. Howard. Calling me doctor wasn't a requirement. Knowing firsthand the personal sacrifices that were made, and the significance of earning a doctorate, was simply enough for me. Does a degree make or break a person? Only time will tell that story.

Ms. Jones was the first person to receive an email from me when the final payment was made. I anxiously awaited her response. When she didn't immediately reply, I made a phone call.

"Ms. Jones, this is doctoral candidate Vanessa Howard. Did you receive my final tuition payment?"

"Let me check the system," she replied. After a moment, she said, "Yes, I see you made your last payment."

My delight in my accomplishments was bursting to leave my closed lips. Using great restraint to keep my "project girl" at bay was a mighty hard task. She wanted to yell from the roof tops, "Bam. Who wasn't going to make the payments on time? What do you think about your better judgement now? There are always exceptions to the rule, and baby you just met her."

Knowing that a simple response would be a better match to my new title, I said, "Thank you for the opportunity to make the payment arrangement. Your support was very instrumental in helping me complete my doctorate. Is my account cleared for graduation? Is there a balance owed?"

She softly said, "Your account shows a zero balance."

Do you know how it felt the moment the last installment payment was made? Celebration time, but this party bus had run out of gas. A surge of happiness radiated throughout my body, knowing that this great financial burden had been alleviated. My eyes had stayed on the prize and my dream of earning a doctorate had been fulfilled.

Squealing loudly with delight, I hung the phone up. Grateful to have completed my two-year journey, my graduation video included appreciation for my family, friends, and the financial aid department.

Chapter 3:

THE LIVING DOLL

Can a human being be a living doll? Growing up in the 1960s and 1970s, it wasn't unusual for African American children to be found playing with affluent White children. My small frame, coupled with my intellect, made me a passable toy. Dark skin that looked smooth like satin, big brown eyes, and long black hair. Large, pouty pink lips that turned red in the wintertime was a bonus to the package. Individuals pay a lot of money for those kinds of lips now.

The Afrocentric toys and dolls that were made in the 1960s were unattractive and made with poor quality materials, so I didn't like to play with them. The dolls of color were stereotypically made with exaggerated features. They had plastic hair painted on their head. Who wants to play with a doll that doesn't have hair to comb?

My parents worked as domestics for rich people. My dad worked on the outside of the houses, cleaning the yards, keeping up the landscape, or cleaning the pools. Mom cleaned their houses, washed clothes, and assisted with household duties as needed. Everyone knew my parents were family-oriented and trustworthy. Having a positive reputation allowed them to secure great gigs with wealthy families in the St. Louis area.

Periodically, Mom would dress me up in my Sunday clothes. She pressed my hair to make me look pretty and made sure those Sunday patent leather shoes were clean. Then I would take long rides with my dad to the homes of their clients to play with their children. Dressing up in my finest clothes made this experience exciting.

The children lived in what appeared to me as mansions. Although starting a friendship with them was easy, it was difficult, when a few months later, our friendship abruptly ended with no explanation. There were times when my dad informed me that we wouldn't be visiting the children's homes anymore. Then, there were several occasions when my friends would abruptly announce the ending of our playtime. They callously said, "My parents said that I can't play with *niggers* anymore."

Weren't we friends? Haven't we been playing together so nicely? What changed?

My parents didn't use the term "*nigger,*" so its true meaning was hidden from me. They didn't talk much about racial inequalities. In our home, conversations about racial inequalities weren't shared with the children. When my older brothers became teenagers, I began listening and learning through their conversations. My dad didn't allow us to mention Malcolm X's name, so my brothers' discussions pulled me like a magnet as my social consciousness was enlightened.

Being born in the 1960s, I was shielded from the racial disparities of the world. My time was spent only around people who loved me and gave me a naïve view of how the world worked at that time. It was incomprehensible to think the interactions I had with the White children weren't real friendships. Spending time in the beautiful homes was a treat. Having the opportunity to participate in tea parties, eat fancy food, and play with realistic looking dolls was a great experience. The floors in the homes we visited were shiny as glass. Walking down their hallway, my heels clicked on the marble floor. With my great imagination, the clicking sounds made me feel like the best tap dancer in the world.

After a while, it became painfully apparent to me that these children were not my friends. They used me as their *living doll*. The pseudo friendships were taking a toll on my self-esteem. Did my parents love their clients more than they loved their daughter?

My dad was the organizer of these trips. On the way to the homes, he strongly encouraged me to be nice to the children. Several times while playing inside with the children, my brothers worked outside cutting these massive lawns with antiquated tools. They used push lawn mowers and sometimes they had motorized units. They trimmed the grass with whatever tools my dad provided. My brothers used their hands to pulled wild weeds out of the ground and in the cracks of sidewalks.

The children were amazed by the texture of my hair and the color of my skin. Believe it or not, those children tried touching my skin to see if they could rub the black off. Why were they perplexed to see a Black child read and write?

In a way, our interactions provided a learning experience for both of us. They learned that we had more things in common than differences. They also discovered that an African American child was capable of being intelligent and articulate. Most of the time, they were inquisitive about my life. They asked a lot of questions about the African American experience. The children began to share their secrets with me. Some of the children spent more time with the nanny than their parents. That made me feel empathy toward them. Some of their parents didn't get along, and there were instances when the children sampled their parents' liquor stash. The amazing thing is that while we were young, our color differences didn't matter to them. However, the older we grew, our relationships became distant.

At one point, I just couldn't endure another moment of these pseudo relationships. Mustering enough courage to have a conversation with my parents was going to take some planning. Finding the right moment to talk to both of them was crucial, so waiting until after dinner was the perfect time. Dad was always in a better mood after supper.

"I don't want to go back to the homes and play with the children anymore," I softly stated.

"Why?" asked mom.

"I'm tired of being nice to kids who don't like me because of my color. Sometimes they call me a nigger and they want to touch me to see if they can wipe the black off my skin. Those kids are not my friends. The way they treat me makes me sad."

My parents nodded and seemed to understand my feelings. My mom looked like she wanted to cry. However, she didn't utter a word. I needed them to explain to me about social justice or racial inequalities. Their silence indicated that this was a conversation they weren't willing to have. But at least my speaking up put a halt to me having to play with their employer's children.

Relieved to be released from *social entanglements*, I was unexpectedly drawn back in for one last time by my neighbor, Mrs. Neal. She told me that she knew a girl named Cindy, who was an only child and was close to my age. Mrs. Neal asked me to come and play with Cindy sometimes.

My answer was no.

"Cindy is lonely, and she is a nice girl. She has trouble making friends," Mrs. Neal said.

Standing my ground, I replied, "No, ma'am."

Back in those days, you had to be careful how you responded to adults. Neighbors could discipline the children of other neighbors. When you got home, your parents would reinforce the lesson all over again. Mrs. Neal said she would give me a quarter for every visit with Cindy. Do you know how much could be purchased with a quarter in the '70s? Yes, became the obvious answer because it meant I would be able to go to the store and buy some candy. Mrs. Neal called my parents to get their approval. What kid wouldn't want to buy their own pack of Now or Laters that they didn't have to share with their siblings?

With Cindy, my strategy was to be the "*boss of her*" and tell her what to do. Cindy was going to follow all my rules. There was nothing to lose since this was a temporary arrangement. When she got to a certain age, we wouldn't see each other anymore.

Mrs. Neal and her husband worked for Cindy's family. Mr. Neal drove the family's car, a Cadillac, or a Lincoln; a luxurious, golden vehicle. Mr. Neal was dressed in his chauffeur attire. His black pants were starched and shiny. He wore a suit jacket with golden buttons, and he placed a shiny patent leather hat on top of his head. He looked and acted like a distinguished gentleman. No one had ever opened the car door for me before. This made me feel like an important person. I sat in the back seat while Mr. Neal chauffeured me to Cindy's house. The ride was so smooth, it lulled me into a light sleep.

When we arrived at Cindy's house, Mr. Neal opened the car door and escorted me to the front door. Mrs. Neal greeted me in a maid outfit. "You look so pretty, Van," she said.

"Thank you," I replied.

Mrs. Neal rubbed my hair and straightened out my bangs. "Cindy is upstairs in her room. You can play there."

I gazed at the beauty of the home. The marble floors were shiny and created the most beautiful checkerboard pattern that I had ever seen. As usual, my church shoes made the familiar tapping sound in the hallway. As we climbed the staircase, Mrs. Neal said, "Cindy is shy. She is a little different, but she's a good girl. She is lonely and just wants to make friends."

Nodding in agreement as we continued up the stairs, I reminded myself, "You are the boss, Vanessa." When we arrived in Cindy's room, she was sitting on a white canopy bed. Mrs. Neal introduced us and left, but before she closed the door, she turned and said, "You girls play nice."

Cindy was frail, and her clothes looked two sizes too big. Her skin was pale and very translucent, exposing blue veins. She hunched her shoulders and wouldn't look at me.

Is she a vampire or something?

Immediately, my tough disposition dissolved. Is this the 'little different' that Mrs. Neal was talking about? Cindy looked younger than me. She also appeared to be afraid of me. How could I be mean to this girl? She looked sick. Maybe that was why Mrs. Neal said she had trouble making friends.

I sat in a chair to assess the situation. Following through with my plan to boss Cindy around might make her cry. If she was sick, she might throw up on me, then my church shoes would be ruined.

Hmm, let me wait until she says something.

Cindy never said anything.

My next option was to wander around and investigate the space.

Cindy had a real tea set made of fine China, not plastic like mine. Stuffed animals were placed all around the room. Having outgrown that phase, those toys couldn't hold my attention. Her bookshelf had so many books, it looked more like a library. They were stacked in neat little rows with stuffed animals decorating the shelves. One book caught my attention. *Alice in Wonderland.* I always wanted to read that story. Pulling the book off the shelf, I heard a soft voice saying, "That's my book."

I froze, waiting for the battle of the wills to begin. "Sorry, I'll put it back."

"You can look at it," Cindy replied.

This was my first experience with a popup book. When the pages opened, the characters were in 3-D. I was in literary heaven. A book filled with surprises and secret compartments. Cindy was no longer the focus; the book had my undivided attention. Time to delve into this masterpiece and read.

"You can read?" she asked, her eyes wide with surprise at this simple feat.

"Yes, I can read,"

Cindy mused, "I didn't know that Black people could read."

My body tensed and my mother's word came into my mind. "Van, think before you speak. You can't always say everything that's on your mind."

"Yes, Cindy, I can read and do a whole lot of other stuff, too."

Cindy dropped her head like she was embarrassed. "I can't read."

That was something new to me, a White kid who couldn't read. My disposition softened towards Cindy. Why would you have a room full of books and not be able to read them? This baffled me, so, my approach with Cindy had to change. "I'll be the teacher, and you listen. Okay?"

Cindy nodded, and her first reading lesson began. Reading the pages first, then showing the pictures to Cindy seemed to keep her attention. This is how my teacher at school read to us. Cindy was a good audience because she clapped at the end of the story.

Mrs. Neal walked into the room with some cookies and milk. "Are you girls ready for a snack?"

We both replied with a resounding, "Yes."

Snack time seemed to help Cindy relax, because she then asked me questions. She asked so many, it became overwhelming. "Where do you live? How many brothers and sisters do you have? Do you have the same parents? What grade are you in?" Before I answered one question completely, she was asking another one.

Dang Cindy! Let's just play for goodness' sake.

Moving around the room became my avoidance tactic. What else in this room would be interesting to do instead of answering juvenile questions? My tactic worked because she stopped giving me the third degree.

In one corner there was a large replica of a house. A doll house that big was a new sight to me. The three-story structure was worthy of my attention, not this lame game show host routine. The doll house had such intricate details that it resembled a mini mansion. The furnishing was much better than my family's furniture. The furniture matched and looked like a magazine photo from Sears and Roebuck. In my house, the furniture in the rooms had different colors and shades. My parents bought what they could afford, and friends and family members gave us the rest of the furniture.

"Man, where is Mrs. Neal? I'm ready to go," I murmured, hoping Cindy didn't hear me. Gazing at the doll house defiantly and glaring side-eyed at her seemed to silence any unwanted conversation.

She didn't speak and we sat quietly in the room until Mrs. Neal came to rescue me.

"Did you girls have fun?" she asked.

Escaping this play date couldn't come quick enough. Nodding then bolting quickly for the door was my way of breaking free. On the way down the steps, Mrs. Neal inquired, "Did you play nice?"

"Yes ma'am."

She gave me the quarter and escorted me to the front door where Mr. Neal was waiting. He opened the car door again. "That was a nice gesture," I thought. The men in my family never opened any type of door for the women.

Children learn a lot when adults are quiet. The trick to finding out what is going on is for kids to be still and pretend to focus on something other than the adult conversations. Kids must be that silent fly on the wall. This invisible posture allows adults to talk freely as if kids weren't present. Eavesdropping revealed that Cindy was a special education student. So that was why Mrs. Neal described Cindy as being a little different.

I empathized with Cindy's plight and was determined to help her. Shifting my focus from bossing her around to becoming her teacher seemed like the best option for both of us. Losing friends is emotionally exhausting. Anyway, my arrangements with Cindy were a temporary diversion.

We played together for several years. Most of our visits were on the weekends during school months and during the summer breaks there were more frequent visits. Having a "*social entanglement*" for several years was surprising. In hindsight, I can attribute the longevity to the fact that Cindy was learning from me and we had mutual respect. She lacked some social skills and wasn't the best reader. Also, she was nervous, she would dig in her nose like she was retrieving gold, then she would eat whatever was on the tip of her finger. This nasty habit was worse than chalk scratching on a board.

Using my mama's voice, she was easily redirected. "Hey. Stop that. Digging in your nose is nasty. Go wash your hands."

Cindy looked startled that I spoke to her in that tone, but she complied and washed her hands. Every time she dug in her nose, she had to wash her hands with soap. It didn't take her long to stop this obnoxious behavior.

My mom taught me to walk with books on my head. She never explained why that was a necessary skill. If my mama taught me, then Cindy needed to learn this skill, too. Since she couldn't read the books, she could practice walking with them on her head until she learned how to read. Cindy really liked this game. We would race around the room to see who could keep the book on their head the longest.

Cindy liked listening to me read. I upped the ante by encouraging her to read along with me. If she didn't know a word, we practiced sounding out the word. Isn't that what good teachers do, show you how to solve problems? Doing this added purpose to my visits.

This *"social entanglement"* didn't end in the best way. Our time together helped Cindy become more confident, and her self-esteem grew. She no longer drooped and hid from the world. She walked tall and upright without using the books. Cindy was a good student and she made me proud of my teaching abilities.

One day, we put the books on our heads like we did in the past. We raced around the room and I won. Although this wasn't my first time winning our book race, Cindy exploded. She didn't use the mama or teacher's voice.

She angrily yelled, "Give me back my book!"

Her reaction was perplexing. What was different this time? We've played that game too long to warrant that type of outburst. She snatched the book off my head and called me a nigger.

That was it. Reaching all the way behind me to add power to my thrust, the book flew quickly across the room, and landed on her face. On her mouth, to be exact.

I bet she would think twice about calling me a nigger again.

Cindy was shocked and immediately turned pale. She covered her lips with a hand and looked at me, immobilized with fear.

Glaring at her eyeball-to-eyeball, I said, "Don't ever call me a nigger again."

It felt freeing to finally release those words. My fists were balled up tightly because it was fight or flight time. No longer would being called a nigger be tolerated.

"You threw a book at me," Cindy cried.

"You called me a nigger."

She sobbed softly and kept looking at me.

Feeling guilty for throwing the book, I responded, "You should never call someone a nigger. Nigger is a bad word to use."

"I heard my parents call you a nigger. So, I called you a nigger, too," Cindy explained.

Over it. After everything that had been done to help their daughter, this is what they thought about me. This time, I exploded, "Yo' mama is a nigger. Yo' daddy is a nigger, and your greasy granny is a nigger, too."

Cindy went from softly sobbing to yelling, "Get out!"

Confused by her outburst, a neck rolling response was necessary this time. "If it's okay for your parents to call me a nigger, then why can't I call your family a nigger, too? That shows me you understand what that word means. So, you can stop faking."

Mrs. Neal came running into the room. When she saw Cindy crying, she immediately shouted at me. "Van, what did you do to Cindy?"

"Cindy called me a nigger."

Assuming Mrs. Neal would be on my side because she was Black was a mistake. Instead, she snatched my arm and dragged me out the room, saying, "Your mama raised you better than that. You embarrassed me."

I knew the routine. Mrs. Neal was going to tell my parents and they were going to give me a whipping. Being disrespectful to Mrs. Neal would cause my disciplining to be worse. So, I accepted her dragging me swiftly down the staircase.

Sitting in the hallway waiting on her husband to take me home, Mrs. Neal continued to reprimand me. "Van, I'm extremely disappointed in you. You can't come back here again."

"But she called me a nigger."

Didn't Mrs. Neal understand? Cindy gained a lot of self-confidence from our time together. She learned how to read, stopped eating boogers, and stopped hunching her shoulders when she walked. The infuriating part was that the only word that her family could use to describe me was nigger.

Well, Cindy can go back to eating boogers. Eat your green and yellow boogers until you throw up.

Surprisingly, Mr. Neal didn't fuss at me. He opened my car door as usual. The ride home was long and quiet. That wasn't my biggest concern. How were my parents going to react when they found out what happened? My brothers taught me that the best defense is a great offense. Diving in headfirst, I immediately told my dad what happened.

He told me he would have thrown a book at her, too. We laughed and that was the finale of my Barbie Doll days.

In retrospect, these experiences caused me to feel "dead from the neck down" when it came to racism and inferiority treatment. It became "normal status quo." Racially insensitive remarks were easy to overlook because they were the "norm." This experience taught me to become desensitized to microaggressions and caused me to overlook racially insensitive behaviors. I had no idea these *living doll* events would prepare me for a major micro assault that could have ended my professional career.

Chapter 4:

HIGHER LEARNING, HIGHER SUFFERING

December 1996 opened the door to financial security. No longer would I be earning less than five dollars per hour with no benefits. Graduating from an HBCU with my bachelor's degree in science helped my self-esteem grow. There was new light and opportunity at the end of my professional journey.

Walking across the stage on this night was simply amazing. My southern belle mom, who only raised her voice when she was upset or angry, proudly yelled, "You go, girl." This phrase still rings in my spirit. She started her higher education quest at thirty and continued it until the day she died.

My mom was my hidden hero. Throughout her life, she demonstrated the importance of education. Before I went to high school, she returned to school to earn her G.E.D. That Mississippi sharecropper woman had grit and tenacity to instill greatness in her only daughter. She completed her associate degree before my high school graduation. We both attended the same university to complete our bachelor's degree. She attended during the day, and I attended at night. Tragically, she died during her senior year, and I continued this educational journey for both of us.

In Missouri, new teachers must earn their master's degree within five years of getting their initial teacher's certification. The state will allow a maximum of eight years for teachers to complete their master's degree to maintain that teaching certification. My goal was to get my advanced degree before the deadline. This university didn't have a reputation for treating minority students fairly. Most African American students flunked out or withdrew from the school, and the retention rate was low. Although horror stories were known throughout the region, their tuition was the most affordable for graduate studies.

In my first statistics class, Dr. Swartz displayed a graph showing how many Black students didn't do well in his class. Dr. Swartz told us that Blacks didn't know how to apply themselves appropriately, and that Black students generally had poor study habits. He proudly proclaimed his theories for all to hear. His class was in an auditorium that housed over thirty students. The six African Americans in this class silently gazed at each other during his presentation, trying to find friendly faces in this uncomfortable situation.

Wow. What a great introduction to graduate school. When I made inquiries with former students in the program, they confirmed that they didn't have a good experience in Dr. Swartz's class. They advised me to wait until the next semester when another teacher was scheduled. But delaying this class a semester would have pushed back my graduation date. I resolved to press forward.

This class tested my learning curve. To adequately prepare for the class, the bookstore recommended a statistical software to assist with completing assignments. To understand the reading materials better, it required reading chapters repeatedly. My confidence in my abilities to master this class had grown, until our first one-hundred-question test. It took the full two hours of class time to complete. I was flabbergasted at my failing score of 44%.

The professor consented when a meeting was requested. When we met, he arrogantly stated, "Didn't I tell you that Blacks can't pass my class? You people just don't read the required text and you don't work with study groups."

"Dr. Swartz, there is nothing in your statement that applies to me. The bookstore recommended a software to help me analyze data. I read the chapters multiple times and used note-taking skills during lectures. What advice do you have for me?"

Dr. Swartz replied, "I see you didn't take time to read my syllabus and see that extra credit assignments are included. Statistics is a difficult course to pass, so extra credit assignments are given to boost grades."

He showed me the section in the syllabus where extra credit assignments are listed. "You can complete as many extra credit assignments as possible to increase your grade point average in my class," he slyly said. I thanked him for his time and began working on a plan of action to pass his class.

At this university, the teachers provided minimal assistance or guidance. They supplied a syllabus and students were responsible for completing assignments without support. Going to a Historically Black College and University (HBCU) is a great experience for minorities. The HBCU goal is to set students up for success by providing tutors and extra support for struggling students. After dissecting Dr. Swartz's syllabus, there was a way to successfully complete his course by turning in all the extra credit assignments. The extra credit assignments would offset poor test scores.

Each week, an additional assignment was turned in. Dr. Swartz pulled me to the side during a classroom break and said, "You know you don't have to do all of the extra credit assignments."

"Since you are giving us the opportunity to complete as many as possible, I'm going to take the opportunity to do them all."

Strategically sitting in the middle of the classroom provided an opportunity to collaborate with the rest of my classmates. Moving out of my comfort zone helped me gain useful tips from other students. After the second test, only two African Americans remained in the class. Dr. Swartz proudly displayed the grade distributions and boasted on how many Blacks had withdrawn from his class.

Several White students rallied around to assist me with successfully completing the course. Privately they shared their displeasure with how Dr. Swartz boasted of the demise of African American students. Although appreciative of their private assistance, I wished they had openly shared their opinions with the instructor.

My new friends helped me to understand formulas and showed me how to create spreadsheets. They also showed me how to analyze student data. They were a godsend.

When we had the midterm, my overall grade point average increased to 73%. The average score was 78%. My plan was working. After this assessment, Mr. Swartz encouraged the class to begin completing the extra credit assignments to boost their final grade point average. "This will be the first time since I have been teaching this class that a student is completing all of the extra credit assignments. She is on track to earn an 'A' in this class if her trend continues," he announced.

The last week of class, there were only twelve survivors and we decided to celebrate this feat by bringing food on the last day. During our celebration, Dr. Swartz let his guard down. He even laughed and talked with us while we ate. At that point, he began to brag about my achievements. My classmates knew my struggles in this class, and they nodded in approval.

After hearing his compliments, I decided to use this as a re-educating moment for the professor. He needed to hear how his microaggression affected students of color. Back-handed compliments aren't an effective tool for anyone. My hopes were that he would take another approach in his initial presentation to future classes.

"I almost dropped your class, but I refused to be a statistic on your board."

Dr. Swartz laughed and said, "Statistics is a hard class to understand. It's difficult to matriculate the formulas and concepts. That's why I created all of the extra credit assignments to balance out grades. You are just the first person to figure it out."

"Dr. Swartz, there were other ethnicities beside African Americans who withdrew from your class. We had a class of thirty; now we are down to twelve. You may want to change your approach when you disaggregate data. Can you imagine someone telling you that because your hair is red, you won't pass their class?"

Dr. Swartz wasn't the only professor who was overly critical of African Americans at this institution of higher learning. They didn't hide behind statistics; they used their words as weapons. African American students couldn't sit with each other. Professors strongly encouraged us to mingle with other cultures and would not start teaching classes until students changed seats. Some professors created seating charts. If an African American resisted or raised objections, security was called to remove that student. Some students were defiant, and their grade suffered because of their noncompliance.

Inquiring minds want to know why I continued to go to this university. I was a working mother and paying for my tuition. My school district gave us pay increases after every six college credit hours. Earning the college hours provided me with two increases in my annual salary, so the system was working. Nothing was going to stop me from providing a quality life for my family.

At this university, I earned two degrees and worked on several other self-improvement classes. Matriculating the ranks helped increase my confidence. The next natural step was to work on my Ph.D. Entry into this doctoral program was daunting. Unsure if this was the right institution, auditing two doctoral classes seemed to be the right path to take.

The doctoral program used Socratic conversations to discuss classroom readings. We sat in a circle and were able to see each other face-to-face. This was a stark difference from sitting in rows. We met in the professor's office and had scholarly conversations. This felt right and it seemed doable. Participating in Socratic conversations was very enlightening. The Ph.D. program was paper-driven and didn't require tests. Writing was my strength. Things were going smoothly.

I strongly considered completing the Ph.D. entry packet, until Dr. Natasha asked me in front of the class, "Vanessa, where did you go to high school?"

This was a St. Louis question meant to reveal your socioeconomic status. When she found out that my K-12th grade experiences were in the city of St. Louis, she looked at me with pity in her eyes.

Her next response shocked me. "Oh, that explains why you talk that way. You are highly intelligent. I can tell by your writings, but the way you speak makes me question the authenticity of your work. Don't you want to do something with your life one day?"

She looked me straight in the eyes, "You need to go to a speech therapist to learn how to talk properly. That's the only way you are going to make something out of yourself."

Even though I was brokenhearted by the callus remarks, there was no support from my classmates.

I wanted to slide under my chair and slither out the door like the invisible man. Why did she say that in front of my peers? So glad I followed my mind and only audited her class. Those comments had a rippling effect on me. They caused me to silence my voice and opinions. No longer was my input included in this class, and childhood stuttering problem resurfaced. Negative thoughts about my dialect consumed me and caused me to transition into a silent participant in class and at work. Dr. Natasha's words propelled me back into a dark hole of despair and self-doubt.

How could I share my thoughts with colleagues? What did my dialect sound like and why did stuttering, my childhood nemesis, reappear?

Chapter 5:

LEADING BY EXAMPLE

Growing up in North St. Louis, I learned to react immediately to avoid becoming a target. Life experiences and counseling have taught me how to process my temper and not be so reactionary. You can be right in your indignation and wrong in the way you respond. Counseling helped me process my feelings in a more positive manner. It also taught me to respond slowly and think before speaking. You will be surprised how effectively you can react when you pause and think. When you express your anger in a professional way, others can hear and relate to your plight. If your reaction is emotionally charged and negative, it will negate all issues at hand. The central point will become how you responded, and the underlying issue will be ignored.

Having gained a reputation for quickly resolving problems and being a master teacher, my district began strategically reassigning me to schools. Teachers are given contracts that guarantee them a position. However, they may be placed in any school building that the district sees fit.

My first teaching assignment was a kindergarten classroom. My principal was a former teacher leader for the Reading Recovery Program. That program provides intervention for primary students who struggle with reading. She encouraged me to become a reading specialist because she saw me skillfully using early literacy teaching strategies.

The district reassigned me to a new school whose principal had an authoritarian leadership style. The school district couldn't find a reading specialist to work in his building because of his assertive disposition. Those assigned to his building frequently requested a transfer or left the school district.

Mr. Maxwell was over six feet tall. His stature, demeanor, and booming voice were intimidating. The staff members shared gossip, that included horror stories of their interactions with him. They told me that my position had been vacant for a year because no one wanted to work with him. *What have I gotten myself into?*

As the school year progressed, I observed Mr. Maxwell more closely to understand his leadership style better. The school was run like a well-oiled machine, thanks to his managerial style of leadership. He had high expectations for the teachers and students, and he wouldn't accept anything less than the best from anyone.

In social settings, you can get a better grasp of a person's true character. Mr. Maxwell consistently completed duty in the cafeteria. Students who owed money or didn't have any cash to pay for their meals were given peanut butter and jelly sandwiches. Mr. Maxwell instituted a policy that all children would be fed a hot meal for lunch. Cafeteria staff kept a tab of how many students needed assistance. Mr. Maxwell reimbursed the cafeteria at the end of the day.

He created a snack drawer for the staff and fed the kids with the monies collected from items sold to the teachers. The staff could buy snacks and he used the money to feed the kids. He also did recess duty with the students and interacted with them informally. *This man can't be that bad.*

When the recess bell rang, the students lined up like soldiers and stood quietly until they entered the building. Mr. Maxwell wanted to make sure they returned to class in a safe and orderly way.

My opinion softened as he demonstrated how much he cared about the kids and how he protected his staff. When staff members or students didn't meet his expectations, Mr. Maxwell would wield the 'power gavel.' No one wanted to get on his bad side. He did not mince words when disciplining staff or students. Several of my colleagues cried after receiving disciplinary actions from him.

We developed a mutual respect over time. We both wanted to give the students the kind of education that they deserved. Since our philosophies of educating children was similar, I volunteered to assist on committees and took the initiative to support wherever there was a need. Mr. Maxwell recognized my leadership skills and encouraged me to pursue an elementary administration certification. He provided opportunities to spearhead projects at the school and I stayed with him for four years before being assigned to another school. My experiences with him taught me valuable leadership lessons.

My next assignment was as a Reading Coach for an elementary school. My role was to train the teachers on providing effective reading instruction by modeling reading lessons, observing teachers, monitoring the data, and assisting the principal as needed. I would have an opportunity to use the administrative skills learned from Mr. Maxwell and other mentors. I was excited to begin this new journey because it came with a $10,000 stipend.

Built in the 1800s, the historic school building was one of the oldest schools in the district. It had three stories and the interior design reflected an older time. The walls were gray, with white pipes prevalent in the ceilings. Most elementary schools were inviting, with vibrant colors displayed around the buildings. Midwest School looked like a prison instead of a facility for molding young minds.

Getting this new assignment had reminded me of the great task at hand. My graduate coursework on working with adult learners would be instrumental to my success. Reading coaches always started the school year before the rest of the teachers. Creating a warm, inviting environment in my office space was crucial. To provide a visual of my goal to be a great coach, a large poster with pompoms was displayed. My heading stated, "I'm your biggest cheerleader."

My hope was that this visual would help the teachers understand that working together, we could help the students learn so much more. To help create a positive rapport with the teachers, they received an introductory email from me that included a mini bio and shared my philosophy of education. The teachers were asked to complete a survey to explain their personal needs and expectation for a coach.

While decorating my office, a teacher came into the room and introduced herself. "Hi, I'm Terry."

Smiling, I replied, "Hi, Terry. It's so nice to meet you."

She handed me the completed survey. After scanning her expectations and nodding at her feedback, I thanked her for completing the survey so quickly.

Terry was a very outspoken person. She asked, "Do you mind if I ask you about your qualifications for this position?"

Startled by the question, my response had to be strategic. "I have been a reading specialist for six years. Certifications by DESE included early childhood, reading, and elementary administration. My reading specialist experiences have included intermediate students and early childhood. In graduate school, additional coursework included early childhood with special education emphasis, and a master's degree in elementary education."

Terry looked amazed by my verbal resume. "I'm just asking because our other reading coach didn't have a reading certification. How could she tell us how to teach reading when she didn't know anything about reading herself?"

Terry left as quickly as she appeared in my office.

Is it customary to ask about the qualifications of your colleague? Should I have returned the favor by asking for her qualifications as well?

Now, my woman's intuition was triggered, giving me warning signs. This wasn't going to be a seamless transition. The principal was very cordial, so my gut feeling had to be wrong. The secretary wasn't as friendly as Mr. Steelman, but once she got to know me better, her disposition should change.

Orientation week had finally arrived. This was the week that staff members return to work to prepare the school for the first day of class. I was eager to meet the entire staff face-to-face and see my new co-workers. When the staff gathered in the library, to my surprise, there was only one African American in the room. That was me. This was shocking to me because the school district student population was predominantly African American. *How is it that this school had such a homogenous staff in a diverse community?*

The staff was pleasant. The younger teachers vibed with me right away. I made a mental note as to how the staff had positioned themselves. The younger teachers sat on one side of the library and the older teachers sat on the other side. People watchers notice these kinds of things. We were all given our building duty assignments. In the morning, my role was to be the front door greeter and to assist with car rider dismissal at the end of the day.

Most effective teachers will use professional attire to model success for their kids. The first sign of respect in the classroom begins with your appearance. Dressing professionally provides a role model for each student. Knowing this fact caused me to become very particular about my wardrobe. Plus, kids make judgements about teacher's personalities based on their clothing and appearance. They act more respectfully toward adults when they dress professionally.

The first day of school was going to be amazing. I was dressed for success and eager to greet the children. The doors opened at 8:30 a.m. Smiling with excitement and ready to receive the young scholars, I said, "*Good morning. Happy first day of school.*" Surprisingly, only a few students returned my greeting.

During the first two weeks of school, teachers generally set the tone for the year by teaching classroom expectations. Wanting to respect the teacher's need to bond with their students and set classroom routines, pop-in visits were used to check on the teachers and to greet their students. Using an informal approach would help me build a better relationship with the teachers. My day was filled with tying shoes, escorting students to the bathroom, and covering the teachers' classrooms so they could get a restroom break, which was a rarity. Teachers train their bladders to go to the restroom at a certain time. You will be surprised that teachers aren't given regular restroom breaks. Restroom breaks are a welcomed treat to teachers.

Every now and then, the backhanded compliments kept recurring. "I wished that our old coach would help us like you," or "I'm so glad you're our coach. You are so much nicer than the previous coach."

The disdain for the previous coach was conveyed with the tone in their subliminal messages. Their comments were placed on my mental shelf to ponder later because my opinion of a person isn't generally influenced by another person's perspective.

The reading coaches had a monthly meeting at central office. There were ten reading coaches for the entire district. When I walked into the room for our first meeting, it was great to have the opportunity to exchange ideas with other reading specialists. Jackie, the coach who was at the school before me, made her introductions first. After our conversation, it became apparent to me this was going to be a rough school year.

Jackie and the other coaches shared horror stories of how she was treated at Midwest School. She was an assertive African American woman who didn't bite her tongue. She had conflict with the staff, and it became a hostile environment. In addition, she had a verbal altercation with one staff member.

Why do I seem to get put in difficult situations? Can't I coast on my job and make easy money like others?

This conversation helped me understand my new placement and the backhanded compliments now made sense. Professional and collegial relationships were in the forefront of my mind. The staff will not get the opportunity to pull me out of my professional character. I wasn't going to be labeled as the "angry Black woman." That label is so freely placed on an African American woman who displays emotions. My goal was to make sure the students had effective literacy instruction.

The best part of the day was greeting the children when they arrived. I continued speaking to them and smiling as they entered the building. Soon they began reciprocating my salutation and returning my smile. Learning students' names became a great way to interact with them. They needed to hear someone call them by their name, to give them hope that their day was going to be fine. Being the greeter also gave me insights into their characteristics and personalities. Some students received hugs and kisses before being dropped off. Certain children weren't adequately clothed for the weather, some wore dirty clothes, and there were other kids in name brand clothing. They wore all kinds of hair styles. It's amazing the variety of ways African Americans can wear their hair.

At times, this school wasn't empathetic to external adversities that affected children's learning. Some parents had untraditional work schedules. If a child was late for school, sometimes it was because the parents got off work late or overslept because of their schedule. My former principal, Mr. Maxwell, made sure that the kids had something to eat. At Midwest school, when students came to school late, they were sent to class without food (based on the cafeteria policy). My preference was to follow Mr. Maxwell's lead and purchase breakfast bars and snacks to keep in my office. When students came to school after the breakfast bell, I offered them a breakfast snack. They ate the snack in my office, then were given a tardy slip and sent to class.

Some of the teachers didn't understand why I let the students come into my office. They didn't like the fact that the students were coming to class late. Because the students who saw me were given a tardy slip, their time was accounted for, which prevented them from getting in trouble. Trying to help the students keep their dignity and self-esteem, the true reason for them spending time in my office was kept secret. Sometimes schools provide the only food that certain students eat.

One day, a boy named Ron in the sixth grade was slapped on his face by his mom. When he noticed that I saw the incident, he stiffened and balled his fist tightly in an aggressive manner. I greeted him normally, but he huffed and tensed up even more. He was on the verge of crying and didn't want his peers to see him get emotional.

Handing him the key to my office, I told him to wait there until my duty was over. When I got there, Ron was sobbing so hard that he couldn't speak. A box of tissue and time to regain his composure was what he most needed.

Suddenly, my phone rang. Ron's teacher was calling. He wanted to know where his student was. I told him told that Ron was helping me unpack a new supply of books. The teacher hung up the phone.

Unsatisfied with my response, he contacted the principal, who in turn came to me.

"Ms. Howard, Mr. Jones said you have Ron in your office," said Mr. Steelman.

Explaining the same thing to the principal didn't help.

"You need to send Ron to his classroom and find another person to help you unpack books. His teacher wants him in class now."

Since I had no choice about letting the youngster stay a little longer to cool off, the only other thing to do was to make him presentable. Ron wiped his eyes and face. Then, we did deep breathing exercises to help him calm down. I unwillingly sent to class, telling him we would catch up during my academic rounds. Ron slowly grabbed his bookbag and went to class.

About ten minutes later, there was a loud commotion. "Get your hands off me. You don't know who you're messing with."

Recognizing Ron's voice, I ran out of my office and toward the disturbance.

Bang. Bang.

Slap.

"Ow."

My legs couldn't move fast enough to get to the loud ruckus that echoed down the hallway. Ron was being escorted down the steps by the principal. He was hitting, kicking, and swinging violently in every direction.

The principal deescalated the situation quickly by treating Ron with respect. He used great restraint as he escorted Ron to the office. He didn't retaliate or defend himself.

Ron was suspended.

As we debriefed, it was revealed that the teacher greeted Ron at the door and immediately started fussing at him because he wore a hat in the classroom. Ron took his hat off, but then Mt. Jones tried to remove his backpack. Taking his frustration out on the teacher, Ron hit him.

The slap Ron had received earlier from his mother created a volatile situation. That's why he needed time to process his feelings. I shared with the principal the interaction I'd witnessed between Ron and his mother, conveying how hurtful it must have been to have her slap him in front of his friends.

During our meeting, the principal disclosed that several teachers had complained about me detaining kids in my office. Needless to say, no one else complained about children being in my office from that point forward.

Physical punishment is used by some parents to enforce discipline. Sometimes, parents use this method to redirect their child's behavior. Research has indicated that when students are physically disciplined, it does not improve behavior and can lead to emotional and academic problems.

I am not advocating for or against physical punishment. However, my support is for giving students time to cool off and work through their feelings with the assistance of an adult. It is imperative for classroom teachers to be observant of their students' dispositions and learn their personalities. Building authentic relationships with kids allows you to immediately know when they are in crisis. Even though the teacher didn't know the specifics of the events that happened prior to Ron's arrival in his class, the child was visibly shaken. He should have been given the common courtesy of a warm greeting when he entered the room, instead of the teacher trying to take his bookbag. Can you imagine what might have happened if the teacher had simply said, "Good morning, Ron. I'm so glad to see you at school."

Chapter 6:

STEP OUTSIDE

Have you ever woken up and thought, *Is this the day to call in sick?* Turns out that this was just that day.

The kids walked quickly into the school to get out of the dreary rain. I couldn't wait to be off duty. The morning was cloudy, damp, and dreary. The walls of the building looked grayer, and a cold draft flowed throughout the building. Watching the clock didn't help. Time moved slowly and the kids were moving fast, causing a cool breeze to send chills down my body.

Whew, it's time to close the door. I couldn't be happier. Turning around to go to my office, a familiar face met me. Ms. Fountain had a scowl on her face and her brows were almost touching each other. That wasn't a great sign. Quickly greeting her and continuing the walk to my office seemed the best course of action.

"I need you to make copies," Ms. Fountain sharply said.

Smiling, I replied, "Did you have your planning period yet?"

Every teacher was given a daily fifty-minute planning period to prepare for lesson activities. During this time, they were to make any copies they'd need for their class.

She shook her head and tried to shove a stack of papers into my hands.

Placing my hands in my pocket, I politely said, "You can use your planning time to make your copies like all the other teachers do. A classroom has scheduled time with me, so you'll have to do it yourself." I turned to walk away.

Ms. Fountain grabbed me by the shoulders and spun me around. This had to be the twilight zone. Somebody had to be playing a trick on me. She shook her wrinkled old finger in my face and yelled, *"Who do you think you're talking to, little girl?"*

Writing this book made me relive that moment. The image of her finger pointing at me is still imprinted in my mind. *Just the thought of it has me feeling some kind of way.*

Let me give you a slower version of what transpired. First, Ms. Fountain touched my body. She physically turned my two-hundred-pound body around to face her. That took a lot of guts and force. She put her pale, wrinkled finger in my face and yelled at me. The staff and students were watching this debauchery. This had to be *fake news*, so I laughed and kept walking, knowing that my next response wasn't going to be pleasant or professional.

Calmly walking away, ignoring Ms. Fountain's ranting seemed like the best thing to do. My silence and calm demeanor should have ended her irrational behavior. However, Ms. Fountain continued to follow me, yelling, "Step outside. I dare you to step outside."

I clenched my teeth, then answered her challenge. "Ms. Fountain, you don't want me to go outside with you."

She yelled, "Yes I do. Step outside."

In my mind, things were happening a little differently. Her wrinkled finger was in my mouth and her blood decorated the gray walls. My fingers itched to wrap around her scrawny neck and stop the air from flowing into her lungs to stifle her annoying screech.

The relationships fostered with my co-workers should have caused me to receive some measure of assistance in halting my tormentor. Instead, several teachers laughed, and the office staff stepped into the hallway to watch this foolishness.

"Little girl, don't you hear me talking to you?" She continued to bark at me like a mad dog.

Where are the cameras? God must surely be testing me. There was no way in the world an institution of higher learning would allow this unreasonable behavior to be displayed in front of children. This had to be a *Candid Camera* moment. I finally understood Jackie's dilemma.

Ms. Fountain's yapping seemed to go on forever. Would this spitting demon stop? Was she related to Linda Blair? She must be the Exorcist's mother.

My colleagues didn't come to my rescue, which left me feeling daunted and alone. The harassment and bullying simply provided entertainment to my peers. How could they allow Ms. Fountain to treat their colleague so disrespectfully? Old insecurities from my *living doll* experiences swept over me as I tried to process this new situation.

I walked quickly to my office and locked the door, then sat in the furthest corner from the entryway and wept. My anger and feelings of betrayal had my body shaking. My goal was to stay out of sight until my emotions were under control. Make-up was going to be my Nubian Queen's mask to walk back into the hostile environment. Dorothy couldn't click her heels and go home. She had to face the music.

Despite the debacle, I kept my normal schedule and checked my mail in the main office. While retrieving my mail, I greeted the office staff as usual. The secretary usually ignored my greeting. Today, she came from around her desk and said, "I thought you were going to hit Ms. Fountain."

A burst of anger rose from my belly to my mouth. My mind wanted to degrade her with cuss words, so smiling was the best option. Reacting negatively wasn't an option because security would have been called to restrain me.

That was the most uncomfortable day I've experienced. Teachers who were chatting and whispering suddenly stopped talking and when I walked past them in the hallways. When the sly looks and whispers became unbearable, the safest place was going to be either my office or my home. Where was my coach, support or even a friend?

The doorknob turned.

I froze. *Oh, hell naw. Ms. Fountain doesn't have to ask me to step outside this time, cause if she steps one foot in this room, it's going down.*

To my surprise, the principal was entering my office.

He shut the door and said, "The staff told me what happened. Ms. Fountain was wrong for yelling at you. Everyone told me that you didn't respond to her. I appreciate you for staying calm."

"Do you realize how much constraint it took not to hit that lady?" I grumbled.

He nodded in affirmative.

"Look, growing up in North St. Louis, you had to be reactive or be the victim. When you ask me to step outside, you're asking me to fight. If I had hit that old lady, you guys would have called the police and had me escorted out of the building." Tears began pouring out of my eyes.

He agreed, hugged me, and walked out of my office. Although that was a nice moment, that wasn't the solution to this issue.

What was going to happen to Ms. Fountain? According to the district policy, staying calm and not being reactive while being harassed was the appropriate thing for me to do. But my tears continued to flow because of the magnitude of her hostility towards me.

I wasn't satisfied with the principal's response, so filing an official grievance was the next step. The assistant superintendent, Dr. Lloyd, came to my school the next day with another central office staff member. They both had sympathetic faces as we began our conversation. They read my grievance and asked for a verbal statement. My statement was void of emotions and stated the facts of the incident. Sometimes when women talk, if we are passionate, men can't hear our words. They only hear the feelings. Simply put, when women display emotions, we are considered irrational.

Dr. Lloyd took the lead in this conversation. "Vanessa, we specifically assigned you to this school because you know how to handle difficult situations. You are more resilient than Ms. Fountain and you are bigger than this situation. Thank you for not responding to her negative behavior."

Sitting motionlessly in a chair, I waited for them to tell me that she would be fired, or she'd received some type of reprimand. "You continue to be strong. Don't let them get to you. We see the students' scores are improving and moving in the right direction. Keep up the good work." Both men left my office.

What kind of pep talk was that? *So, I'm just here to be abused, harassed and dragged around like a puppet?* This wasn't the resolution that I had hoped for.

The principal and I met after the assistant superintendents left. He addressed my concerns by saying, "Talking about the discipline of another staff member is prohibited by board policies. Just stay out of Ms. Fountain's room until she calms down."

What the what?

Acting professional didn't seem to work in my favor. Being annoyed by the lack of support caused me to groan loudly. "Things would have turned out differently if the roles had been reversed. The police and security would have been called if a Black woman was the aggressor. I would have been dragged out of the building with handcuffs. How do you think this makes me feel? The way she yelled at me in front of the students and the teachers was unprofessional and antagonistic. Ms. Fountain physically turned my body around to face her and pointed her finger in my face. When she asked me to step outside, she was implying that she wanted to do me bodily harm. That's considered assault."

He shook his head sympathetically. "Believe me, I understand exactly how you feel. However, board policy prohibits me from sharing the discipline of other employees."

Do you want to know what happened to Ms. Fountain? Nothing happened. Ms. Fountain came to work every day. Following the principal's instruction was going to be easy. My presence was null and void in her room for the remainder of the school year. My communication with her became non-verbal. We exchanged nods and quick waves in the hallway or in staff meetings to maintain a courteous and professional working environment.

Several staff members privately commended me for using restraint during her verbal assault. It would have been nice to have heard this publicly. For the next year and a half, my emotions were at work every day to prevent any more betrayals of trust. As soon as the opportunity presented itself, I transferred from that school.

Chapter 7:

NIGER VS. NIGGER

Have you ever received a text message from your supervisor before work hours, asking about a project you completed? My supervisor, Sally, texted me to send her a copy of the curriculum project that I had just completed. The document was shared with her in Google drive the night before. Relaying that to her should have ended the exchange.

It didn't.

The next text I received stunned me.

Sally's message stated, "I no longer like niger."

I was speechless. To me it read, "I no longer like niggers."

How do you respond to a text like that? There was no reasonable reply to make. This had to be an error.

Who was she texting?

My old insecurities began to resurface as I dressed for work. Driving to work was challenging. The text left me feeling outraged and insulted. How many more times would racism rear its ugly head in my life? Turning into the driveway of the school district, my heart rate and breathing patterns accelerated. Slow breathing exercises while walking into the building assisted in calming my nerves.

When I arrived at about 7:45 a.m., Sally was talking to one of my colleagues by my desk. *Really. Considering the text, you sent me, you have the audacity to be standing by my desk.* Sally was laughing with colleagues. "I can't believe I sent that message to Vanessa."

She repeated the story, adding a nervous laugh at the end. "This morning, I was dictating a text to Vanessa and it typed in niger. I meant to say, 'I no longer had access to the folder.' Can you believe the phone typed niger?"

My supervisor and colleagues laughed again. They looked at each other while they chuckled. This joke wasn't funny. Why should they feel comfortable making an inappropriate comment? The anger inside of me swelled and rumbled. Instead of responding, I searched inside my computer bag for my headset to drown out this foolish banter.

Then my supervisor asked, "Vanessa do you hear me?"

The best thing at that moment was to ignore Sally's question and drown out the sound of her voice with music. The melody blasted loudly in my ears as anger spewed out of every pore in my body. Working vigorously on my next task redirected my thoughts.

Why is it that when an African American woman is irritated, their emotion is categorized negatively? Who coined the phrase angry Black woman? My initial response would have been characterized as bad-tempered, hostile, or overly aggressive.

Soon, they walked away from my desk, looking at me strangely, as if I was the one who had done something offensive. "Oh, it's okay. I know you made a mistake," was what they wanted to hear. Being called a nigger makes you feel completely dumbfounded, hurt, powerless, and angry, all at the same time. It leaves a psychological wound the same way a scar leaves a scab. There is always a reminder of the pain.

Sally went around the office telling people her joke.

How could anyone find the situation humorous when the connotation of the word nigger is so negative and hurtful?

Later, I shared the text with a Black colleague to hear another perspective. Her response was unbelievable to me. She simply stated that she didn't think Sally was racist, and that she didn't' mean me any harm.

No harm. Did you read the text?

"Vanessa, she isn't calling you a nigger. It's not spelled right," she replied.

She looked the word up in the dictionary and showed me that Niger is a country in West Africa.

"If she felt she had made a mistake, then instead of talking to my colleagues, Sally should have had a private conversation with me."

Prior to this incident, I had a great professional relationship with my team. My evaluations were excellent, and the Assistant Superintendent often praised me. After this incident, Sally began nitpicking my work.

Seeking assistance was no longer an option. It was now a career necessity. At that time, we had an interim African American Superintendent. She was our former Human Resource director. If anyone knew the correct procedures to follow, she would be the one person to have the right solution. A meeting was scheduled for us.

When Dr. Young saw the text, she was immediately enraged and wanted to confront Sally. Fearing retaliation and being unfairly targeted by Sally made me hesitant to respond. My past experiences with racism caused me to be desensitized to racial biases. My coping mechanism was to ignore and suffer in silence.

The Superintendent took out her cell phone and dictated a text. "I no longer have access to the folder."

She showed me the results. "Do you see niger on my text?"

"No."

She then used the transcription feature for the second time, saying the phrase 'no longer.' She asked, "Do you see niger now?"

"No."

Dr. Young explained that when you use a word frequently on your phone, the voice recorder will remember that term and use it. Dr. Young's text transcribed her words verbatim.

Why was I scared of retaliation when Sally was the offending person? Previous experiences had taught me to feel voiceless and isolated.

The interim superintendent was leaving at the end of the school year. If she intervened, there was a strong possibility of retaliation. Being the sole provider for my family, there was no financial exit plan, so leaving at that time was not a viable choice.

Dr. Young helped me craft a letter to the assistant superintendent who was responsible for my department. She told me to request a meeting, read my letter, and share how the incident made me feel.

I went back to my desk and Dr. Young followed me. She put her arm around my shoulders and told me to keep her informed. She walked past Sally's desk and glared at her as though her eyes were fiery darts.

Following Dr. Young's advice, I typed the letter and sent it to the assistant superintendent, who scheduled a meeting among the three of us. Confronting my abuser made me extremely nervous. When you have been victimized for years, you become conditioned to being a target. The superintendent gave me the tools necessary to face Sally.

This was a big step.

Meeting day finally arrived. My anxieties were high, and tears welled up in my eyes. Blinking slowly kept them from falling. Several trips to the restroom to pray helped me gain my composure. Lack of moral support from co-workers led me to stay silent about the meeting.

They wouldn't understand my grievance. Plus, they hadn't supported me when the incident was presented as a joke.

When it was time, Dr. Pearson came to my cubicle to get me. At that point, my co-workers realized what was transpiring. As we walked to the conference room, it seemed as if the sound of my shoes became a visual magnet for my co-workers.

Dr. Pearson started the meeting acknowledging my letter. She gave us the rules she was using to mediate this meeting. Both of us were given a chance to explain our side of the story. I shared the text and explained how Sally discussed personnel information about me with another staff member.

"The conversation she shared made me feel devalued and uncomfortable because they were laughing at her using a racial slur against me. Being called a nigger is very hurtful. The text stirred up some past wounds and made me feel degraded. Now, it feels like Sally is targeting my job performance because I found no humor in her inappropriate joke."

Sally presented next, saying, "Vanessa was working on a file that she was supposed to share with me. Using the dictation feature on my phone in haste, the text was transcribed incorrectly and sent before it was spell checked. The only reason I shared my mistake with Tina was because I felt so awful. Vanessa wouldn't talk to me about it. She ignored my attempts to have a conversation. Since that incident, Vanessa has had an attitude with me, and her work performance has declined."

Dr. Young's advice about stressing that supervisors should not share personnel information with another person who was not directly involved in an incident helped me find the courage to speak further.

"If you were embarrassed by your email, you should have spoken to me privately. I didn't understand why you would share your miscommunications with my colleagues. The term nigger is very hurtful.

Having been called that before made me feel uncomfortable laughing at your inappropriate joke. That's why I put on the earphones to drown out the upsetting emotions you stirred up in me."

Dr. Pearson asked whether we felt we could continue having a positive working relationship. We both agreed. She assured me that I was a great asset to my department and complimented me on bringing new energy to the school district. She said, "I feel like you guys have had a misunderstanding."

We both agreed.

The meeting was adjourned with no apology offered or implied.

Eventually, we got a new superintendent and Dr. Pearson received a promotion in a different school district. Guess who took Dr. Pearson's place? Sally received that promotion. Did things get better in my working relationship with Sally? No.

Dr. Young gave me the tools to empower me to stand up to racism. I was fortunate to find a therapist who was a former superintendent of a school district. He was very instrumental in helping me discover my voice and helped me to re-build my self-esteem. He helped me learn how to be an advocate for myself and showed me how my unresolved trauma had affected my decision making.

Although I had learned to navigate difficult transitions and issues in this district, I became keenly aware that searching for a new position had become a priority.

Chapter 8:

TEACHER OF THE YEAR

Many teachers discover that their love of children draws them to teaching, or that their own love of learning makes them passionate about teaching. It never crossed my mind that someone would recognize me for doing what I love. Teaching can be a thankless position, one that is overlooked and underrated.

While in graduate school, I met a nice lady, and we became friends. Her school district was adding a new primary wing, so they were opening a new kindergarten section. She gave my name to the principal. The principal had Human Resource pull my application for an interview. Before the first round of interviews, the assistant superintendent greeted me and explained, "We are on a strict timeline because we have a lot of candidates to interview. You only have three minutes to answer every question."

To me, the interview went great. As requested, the questions were answered within the three-minute timeline.

The next day, the principal called. "You've made it to the second round of interviews. But it was a tough sell because you gave short answers. Take your time and answer all parts of the questions next time. You rushed through your responses and almost didn't make the final cut."

Using her advice to answer the questions more thoroughly helped me get the position.

The principal walked me to my car and said, "Rob said I was foolish to hire you and that you wouldn't be a good teacher because you didn't know how to answer basic teaching questions. Their loss is my win. Welcome to my school."

Rob was the assistant superintendent for human resources. He was the person that told me to give brief answers. This was a valuable lesson. Listen intently to interview questions, elaborate on your responses, and support your answers with an example.

The position at the new school district provided a $13,000 yearly increase in my salary. My tenure in this district was fifteen years. I served on numerous district-level committees and played intricate roles throughout that region. This might shock you, but during my fourteenth year in the district, over 2,000 of my fellow employees voted me Teacher of the Year. This project girl was the third African American Teacher of the Year in the history of the district. What an awesome feat. My picture still hangs on the wall of the school boardroom.

Want to know something else? That same year, the *St. Louis American Newspaper* awarded me the Excellence in Education Award. There were several feature articles about me in the newspaper. This award came with money and a certificate for diamonds from a jeweler. Only God can take a girl from the projects to the boardroom.

If you aspire for greatness, with perseverance you can reach your goals. Never give up on your dreams.

Chapter 9:

PERFECT FIT

Have you ever found a great body shaper that made you look like you had an hourglass figure? It hugs all your curves and hides the unsightly lumps. With an effective body shaper, you can't tell me nothing because my issues are hidden, and my best self is on display. Finally got my body shaper job. The position was tailored to my strength, fit me in the right places, and helped me to shine in the best light possible. Everything fit perfectly and my lady lumps and bumps were well hidden.

In 2020, I decided to leave the public school system and work for a corporation. This job was tailor made for my skill set, life experiences, and personality. Although there are only two African Americans on staff, the organization is culturally responsive to all employees. This company's philosophy is that employees should be given everything they need to be successful and that quality time with family is paramount. Happy employees are the best employees. No more 10-to-14-hour workdays.

I am a nationwide presenter for the company and my picture was chosen for a national ad campaign. Meet Dr. V. She is a fifty-six-year-old print model. It's as if God reached down from heaven and created this. Many were interviewed, but two people were hired. My professional experiences prepared me to successfully transition into this new appointment.

Taking this position meant I'd be accepting a twenty-five-thousand-dollar pay cut. But all money isn't good money. At fifty-six years old, peace of mind is more valuable than the coins. Like the Bible says, if you are faithful over a few things, He will make you ruler over many. The retirement plan with this company is lucrative. Upon retirement, my pension will be almost one thousand dollars greater than the public school system pension. With this company, family is truly first. God looked down and decided to give me double for my trouble.

You are probably asking yourself why I wrote this book. The accounts contained on these pages are intended to help people develop compassion and consideration for others. When you think about the human race, we have evolved, and accomplished many great feats. We sent men to the moon and developed technological systems that would rival Ben Franklin's discovery of electricity. None of these great accomplishments were achieved by a single person. The secret is that although we all have developed some inherent biases over time, many of us suppress those tendencies for the good of society.

Fear has been known to trigger unfair biases. However, developing empathy and keeping an open mind to varied viewpoints can help build bridges instead of walls. The human disposition is both genetically and environmentally influenced, and if we stay in our social bubble, it will be difficult to alleviate fear or distrust. Each individual needs to choose whether they will tolerate and trust someone, or fear and reject them. That choice is influenced by culture. The individuals around us say and do things subconsciously that influence the way we think. When individuals we trust talk a certain way, it becomes our norm.

Acknowledging your biases is the first step to cultivating the ability to have consideration for others. It takes twenty-one days to learn a new habit. If you never get out of your comfort zone, you'll never learn to appreciate the uniqueness and beauty of humanity. When we understand that our "hardwired" urges are unhelpful in the context of culture, we can develop positive social interactions.

We can change our own behaviors by expanding our immediate social circle. Doing so will help us begin to understand and validate the differences between various cultures. Most importantly, now that you are aware of some cultural preconceptions, you can no longer be silent. If you see racism, call it out. Let your co-workers, family, and friends know that it isn't appropriate. Microaggression can appear in the form of racist jokes or statements that are normalized and very prejudiced in nature. Being silent or laughing along with the jokes mean that you agree with the comments.

We can reinforce positive values, build trust, and compassion, and reduce the distinction between cultures. We need to have courageous conversations. Let's retrain ourselves to find the good in people. Open yourself up to discovering the things that bind us together as a human race, instead of focusing on those that keep us apart. Although we cannot totally eradicate racism, we can make a better tomorrow for our children and our children's children.

I have learned to use my voice and express myself when statements or actions make me feel uncomfortable. Suffering in silence or ignoring your feelings can misdirect your emotional state. It's okay to say, "You make me feel devalued when …" or "You make me uncomfortable when you say …" Putting the offending party on notice in a professional manner is the first step to recovering your dignity. Even if your comments are ignored, you will no longer be a victim.

Counseling has also helped me process my feelings and emotions. Therapy helped me regain my voice and showed me how my traumatic upbringing shaped the way I interacted with people. Therapy taught me ways to deal with my work apprehensions and how to communicate more effectively.

Do you remember the professor that suggested that my speech was impeding my professional progress? Her comments were humiliating, and the sting of her cruel darts had a rippling effect on my self-esteem. Her comments caused me to be reluctant to speak in large groups, made me fear my dialect, and created anxieties that my childhood stuttering might resurface at the wrong time. My next self-improvement plan was to get a speech therapist to help me articulate my words better. The therapist assured me that she had no concerns about my speech pattern. The only recommendation given was to practice tongue twisters to assist me with experimenting with language.

My journey of self-improvement included weight management, higher learning, speech therapy, and counseling, based on the recommendations of others. My children are grown, and I have one granddaughter. I am a divorcee, and my life didn't end because of the divorce. Today, I accept me and love myself, *flaws, and all*.

Chapter 10:

COURAGEOUS CONVERSATIONS

Have you heard the term "cultural responsiveness?" It is the ability to learn from and relate respectfully to people in your culture, as well as those who aren't from your culture. It is a good practice to be aware of because it causes you to respect the point of view of other individuals, even when they differ from your opinion. Am I saying that you should agree with everyone? Absolutely not. Respecting differing opinions simply means being willing to recognize that we have different viewpoints. Tolerance enables us to be able to treat each other with mutual respect.

For example, in 2005 during the Hurricane Katrina disaster, the media (including The Associated Press, *The New York Times,* and other news organizations) classified African Americans that were displaced due to a natural disaster as refugees. The implication was that victims of the hurricane, who were predominantly African Americans, were second class citizens and not Americans. Eventually, the term was dropped when referencing hurricane victims.

Each cultural group develops a shared form of communication. I call it "Home Language." This specially designed form of language or communication creates a safe sense of belonging. Not understanding the nuances of language can create barriers and misunderstandings between differing cultures. The language that is developed or created evokes emotions. Home language is used when you have difficulty expressing your thoughts using standard English. When a person is emotional, they generally resort to their home language.

Culture directly impacts the way its members communicate. Social norms are created and generally shape the way each person in the group communicates. As humans, we want that authentic experience with a person. I am going to share with you several strategies to assist you in effectively communicating across cultures.

1. Know yourself and be aware of your biases (conscious and subconscious).

2. Develop authentic relationships around mutual interests. Focus on what you have in common.

3. Don't rush to judgement or generalize a culture. Never say *never* and never say *all*.

4. Stay authentically true to your character. Don't pretend to be part of different cultures because you have gained some knowledge about the people. Being pretentious alienates others, and it can easily be detected.

5. Say something when you see someone being discriminated against. Silence and laughter mean you agree.

6. Go outside your comfort zone and talk to people from other cultures. You will be surprised how much you may have in common.

7. Validate a person who may have been hurt or discriminated against. This will help them know they aren't alone and hopeless.

8. Converse with your co-workers and neighbors. Exchanging cordial greetings or pleasantries with a person doesn't hurt. You are just acknowledging a human being and letting them know that someone 'sees' them. Don't walk by co-workers and not speak, especially if this is a person you see frequently. This type of behavior builds walls of separation.

9. Use your own home language. Don't try to code-switch when you speak to someone of a different culture. This can seem pretentious, and it can be very annoying.

10. Be open minded to differences you may see.

I hope that the experiences shared will give you the tools needed to make your life's journey a little easier. I challenge you to start having meaningful conversations with someone from another race, socioeconomic background, religion, individuals with disabilities, or sexual orientation. You will find that we have commonalities and interesting uniqueness. Instead of letting our differences build bridges, we can let our diversity unite us for the common good of mankind.

Dr. Vanessa Howard,

affectionately known as Dr. V, is an award-winning educator and author. She started her writing career creating stories for children in her classroom. Her high interest reading materials were instrumental in helping students develop a love for reading. Dr. V has written a memoir, *From Projects to a Ph.D.: A View from the Other Side of America*, to provide cultural awareness to racial biases and its detrimental impact on minorities.

Her other projects include Christian, contemporary, and women's fiction, as well as paranormal stories, and non-fiction books that focus on relationships and women's issues. Currently, she teaches at university level and is a nationwide speaker and literacy trainer. In her spare time, she likes to sew and spend time with her family.

Find her on the web atwww.drvanessahoward.com
Website: www.drvanessahoward.com
SocioTap: https://sociatap.com/Drvhoward/

50 Days of Pleasure

VANESSA HOWARD

FROM THE PROJECTS TO A PH.D.

A VIEW FROM THE OTHER SIDE OF AMERICA

DR. VANESSA HOWARD

Things
that keep me up at
Night

A Memoir

Marie McKenzie

Single Again?

HOW TO LIVE
SATISFIED UNTIL ...

Erica B. Davis

Growing UP

Joplin

KADESHA POWELL

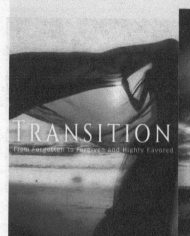

TRANSITION
From Forgotten to Forgiven and Highly Favored

USA TODAY BESTSELLING AUTHOR
NALEIGHNA KAI

VISION
Aligning With God's Purpose For Your Life

NATIONAL BESTSELLING AUTHOR
J.L. CAMPBELL

JOURNE
Finding God's Path For Your Life

NATIONAL BESTSELLING AUTHOR
LISA DODSON

GROWTH
Extraordinary Lessons from Ordinary Occurrences

NATIONAL BESTSELLING AUTHOR
JANICE M. ALLEN

CHOICES
Standing in the Gap or Standing in the Way?

NATIONAL BESTSELLING AUTHOR
PAT G'ORGE-WALKER

PERSISTENC

U.M. HIRAM

PURPOSE
Life According to God's Plan

FLORENZA DENISE LEE

PATIENCE
Persevering Through the Wait

NATIONAL BESTSELLING AUTHOR
TERRI ANN JOHNSON

TRANSFORMATIO
From Broken to Blessed

NALEIGHNA KA

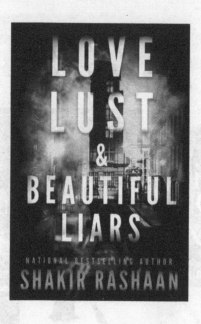

Dorian Bentley is the top international arms dealer in the world. His customers only know him by his moniker—The Wraith—a revenant whose trail is difficult to trace by government law enforcement authorities.

He has begun to cultivate his endgame, one that will have him turn over his expansive empire to one of his lieutenants and retire an ultra-rich man. He needs time—time he may no longer have—before everything comes crashing down.

Samara D'Acosta, the woman he'd given his heart too long ago—despite keeping her at arm's length for her own protection—is a part of those plans, but will her own secrets derail their happy ever after?

Love, Lust & Beautiful Liars is the latest explosive tale from national best-selling author, Shakir Rashaan, where the lines between lust and love blur, and where no one is who they seem.

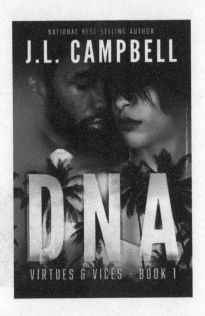

What can go wrong when an ambitious man accepts a promotion overseas without consulting his wife?

Much more than Russell Majors anticipates.

With a thriving career, a comfortable home, and two healthy sons, this new chapter is an unwelcome surprise for Amoy Majors.

A move abroad means physical exams, biometric screenings, and embassy interviews. All normal requirements, or they would be, if she didn't believe they might stir a hornet's nest.

When an unauthorized test yields unexpected results, the pillars on which her life is built are shaken.

Whether her marriage will survive a shocking revelation, and her faith withstand a trial by fire, is anyone's guess.

Who goes through life without bruises and knockdowns? No one. But do you know who comes out on the other side with healing and strength? Those who make up in their minds that they want a different way of experiencing life. The good news is that there's no reason why you can't be that person.

The Bible says that the steps of a good man or woman are ordered by the Lord. But sometimes those steps take us down a road of pain, disappointment, misfortune, and trials that we would not have chosen for ourselves. It's at these times that we can experience tremendous growth by allowing God to work all things (even unpleasant things) together for our good.

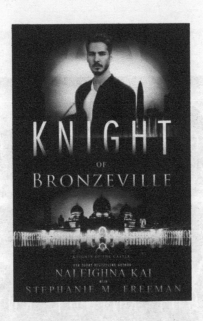

Chaz Maharaj thought he could maintain the lie of a perfect marriage for his adoring fans ... until he met Amanda. The connection between them should have ended with that unconditional "hall pass" which led to one night of unbridled passion. But once would never satisfy his hunger for a woman who could never be his. When Amanda walked out of his life, it was supposed to be forever. Neither of them could have anticipated fate's plan.

Chaz wants to explore his feelings for Amanda, but Susan has other ideas. Prepared to fight for his budding romance and navigate a plot that's been laid to crush them, an unexpected twist threatens his love and her life. When Amanda's past comes back to haunt them, Chaz enlists the Kings of the Castle to save his newfound love in a daring escape.

For your reading pleasure

CPSIA information can be obtained
at www.ICGtesting.com
Printed in the USA
LVHW040326070721
691973LV00008B/689

9 781736 698709